# The Rise and Fall of the Democra

## SPEECH

OF

# HON. KINSLEY S. BINGHAM,

## OF MICHIGAN.

Delivered in the United States Senate, May 24, 1860.

Mr. PRESIDENT: The resolutions under discussion were presented by the honorable Senator from Mississippi, [Mr. DAVIS,] one of the most distinguished and worthy leaders of the Democratic party. It is understood that they have been adopted by a large majority of Democratic Senators in caucus; and although they have not been formally voted upon by the Senate, yet I think it fair to presume that they express the opinions and embody the creed, not only of the majority of this honorable body, but of the dominant party in the country. The honorable Senator from South Carolina, [Mr. CHESNUT,] in his discussion of them, says that they "are just, and therefore wise. In regard to the subjects of which they treat, they announce the true doctrine of the Constitution. Among other things, they denounce two capital political heresies: that which claims sovereign power for the Government—unlimited power—over this subject, and that which claims sovereign power for the inhabitants of a Territory." The fourth and fifth resolutions are in the following words:

"4. *Resolved*, That neither Congress nor a Territorial Legislature, whether by direct legislation or legislation of an indirect and unfriendly nature, possess the power to annul or impair the constitutional right of any citizen of the United States to take his slave property into the common Territories; but it is the duty of the Federal Government there to afford for that, as for other species of property, the needful protection; and if experience should at any time prove that the Judiciary does not possess power to insure adequate protection, it will then become the duty of Congress to supply such deficiency.

"5. *Resolved*, That the inhabitants of an organized Territory of the United States, when they rightfully form a Constitution to be admitted as a State into the Union, may then, for the first time, like the people of a State, when forming a new Constitution, decide for themselves whether slavery, as a domestic institution, shall be maintained or prohibited within their jurisdiction; and if Congress shall admit them as a State, 'they shall be received into the Union with or without slavery, as their Constitution may prescribe at the time of their admission.'" *

The party now known as the Democratic party has been a distinct organization more than sixty years, and is almost coeval with the foundation of the Government. Looking for its paternity to the author of the Declaration of Independence, the immortal Jefferson, the Democratic party has ever claimed to be the advocate of the largest liberty; of the greatest good to the greatest number; of equal rights and equal privileges; of a strict construction of the Constitution; and in favor of State rights, in opposition to the powers claimed for the Federal Government by the Federal party. The Democratic party has professed opposition to all monopolies—all exclusive privileges; and two of its great leaders, Jefferson and Jackson, took open and strong ground against the political decisions of the Supreme Court, which were designed to control the legislation of Congress, or to affect the judgment or conscience of its individual members; but never, previous to the year 1846, did the Democratic party, or any of its leaders, deny the power of Congress to legislate exclusively for the Territories, and especially to prohibit the introduction of slavery therein.

* These resolutions have since passed the Senate, but one Democrat (Mr. Pugh) voting against them.

Immediately after the close of the Revolutionary war, Mr. Jefferson announced the great principles of civil polity which were to lie at the foundation of the new States, to be formed out of what was then the only Territory they possessed; and in 1787, they were formally adopted by Congress, in the promulgation of the ordinance which prohibited the introduction of slavery therein. Every new settler, as he crossed the border of that great Territory, to establish for himself and his children a home, had the solemn assurance of the Government that free labor was never to be degraded by its contact with slavery upon that soil, and that free men could only live there.

I shall undertake to show, Mr. President, that this benign policy, the salutary effects of which will be acknowledged as long as we respect the virtues of our ancestors, was the policy of the Government under the new Constitution, and especially of the party first known as the Republican, and afterwards as the Democratic party; and that the Republican party of to-day only desires to carry out the principles which were adopted by the Republican party of 1800, and by the enforcement of which the present flourishing States of Ohio, Indiana, Illinois, Michigan, Wisconsin, Iowa, and Minnesota, have sprung. One of the first acts, under the new Constitution, voted for by many of the men who had come fresh from the Convention which framed that instrument, was approved, on the 7th of August, 1789, by General Washington; and the preamble is in these words:

"Whereas, in order that the ordinance of the United States, in Congress assembled, for the government of the Territory northwest of the river Ohio, may continue to have full effect, it is requisite that certain provisions should be made, so as to adapt the same to the present Constitution of the United States."

Here is a complete recognition of the power of Congress to legislate for the Territories, and to exclude slavery therefrom; for this act re-enacted and re-established the provisions of that ordinance. In pursuance of the policy marked out by the ordinance to which I have referred, Congress, from time to time, in the organization of Territorial Governments, applied the same restriction of slavery by direct legislative enactment; and so unquestioned was the complete power of Congress over the subject, that, in 1802, President Jefferson approved the enabling act authorizing the people of Ohio to form a State Government, which contained a proviso that the Constitution should not be repugnant to the ordinance of 1787. Mr. Madison approved a similar act, in relation to Indiana, in 1816, and Mr. Monroe one relating to Illinois, in 1818. Acts were passed during the Administration of every Democratic President, down to and including James K. Polk, when the Territory of Oregon was organized, with the same prohibition, that there should be "neither slavery nor involuntary servitude in said Territory, otherwise than in the punishment of crime, whereof the party shall have been duly convicted." During all this period, Congress not only exercised the power unquestioned of prohibiting the existence of slavery in the Territories, and of requiring the State Constitutions to conform to the provisions of the ordinance, but it exercised the power of *regulating* slavery in the Southwestern Territories.

Under the provisions of the Constitution, Congress could not restrain the foreign slave trade until the year 1808, and that infamous traffic was regarded as legitimate commerce. And yet, in 1794, Congress discriminated against this species of property, and prohibited the carrying of slaves to any foreign country, and utterly condemned slaves and slavery as an article of commerce. In 1798, ten years before Congress had authority to prohibit the importation of African slaves into the States, in the act for the government of the Mississippi Territory, the seventh section makes it unlawful to bring slaves into the Mississippi Territory from any place without the United States; imposes a fine of $300 for every slave thus brought into the Territory in violation of the provisions of the act, and gives to every slave thus brought in, his or her freedom. The doctrine of "*non-intervention*" had not been invented at that time, and the Congress of that day was not hindered by constitutional scruples from exercising the sovereign power of prohibiting the African slave trade in the Territories ten years before they were authorized to make the same prohibition in the States.

In 1804, when the Louisiana Territory was organized, similar provisions were enacted, prohibiting the introduction of slaves into the Territory from any place without the United States, with an additional provision against the introduction of any slaves from the States, that had been imported since 1798, exercising unquestioned, express authority to prohibit and regulate slavery, and all other matters, in the Territories. These acts were approved by Jefferson—authority which the Democratic party has never had the hardihood to dispute. Congress afterwards, in the year 1836, repealed and nullified the Territorial acts of Florida incorporating certain banks and insurance companies, and this act received the sanction of General Jackson. Congress also, in several instances, legislated in relation to slavery in Florida.

In the year 1800, a petition from Mississippi Territory was sent into Congress, praying for permission to take slaves into the Territory. This petition was introduced into the House of Representatives. The House passed a bill entitled, "An act to permit, in certain cases, the bringing of slaves into the Mississippi Territory."

This Territory was at the southern extremity of the United States, and altogether surrounded by an old slaveholding population. The bill passed the House without a division. It was sent to the Senate, where Thomas Jefferson presided, he being Vice President, where it was rejected by a vote of 14 to 5.

From this statement it will be seen, Mr. President, that for a long period in the history of the Government, and of the Democratic party under its most distinguished leaders, the power of the Government over its Territories, in all respects, was unquestioned; and that the wise and statesmanlike policy of restricting and regulating slavery was invariably pursued.

But, "then arose a new king which knew not Joseph." The precepts and example of Jefferson were discarded. An influence appeared in the Southern States, which sought to change the settled policy of the Government, and to establish and perpetuate the institution of slavery. This influence I shall denominate the slave power. Perhaps its first attempt to control the Democratic party was in the nomination of President in 1844. Having acquired a large additional strength by the admission of the States of Louisiana, Missouri, Arkansas, and Florida, from territory acquired by treaty and purchase, this same power undertook, very adroitly, to precipitate the question of the annexation of Texas into the Presidential canvass of that year, and to commit the Democratic party to that measure. Mr. Van Buren was a prominent candidate for nomination at the Baltimore Convention; and it was known that, during his Presidency, he had rejected proposals for the annexation of Texas, while Mexico refused to acknowledge her independence, and hostilities existed between those two Republics. As a pretext for defeating his nomination, a letter was thereupon addressed to Mr. Van Buren, inquiring whether he favored the present annexation of Texas. He replied, in manly and statesmanlike terms, that although he did desire the annexation of Texas, he could never consent to the measure at the expense of involving us in a war with our sister Republic of Mexico, between whom and this Government there existed a treaty of peace and friendship. The publication of the letter produced the desired effect; and, amidst great excitement, the nomination of Mr. Van Buren was defeated, and James K. Polk became the candidate of the party. This was an open and signal triumph of the slave power; and resolutions were passed in favor of the immediate annexation of Texas.

The discipline of the Democratic party was at that time rigid and exact; but now and then a brave and honest man, like my friend from New Hampshire, who sits near me, [Mr. HALE,] refused submission to its dictation, and openly opposed the annexation of Texas. There was danger of a general outbreak in the party, and something must be done to allay their fears. At that conjuncture, Mr. James Buchanan, then a Senator of the United States, and then, and ever since, the willing and supple instrument of the slave power, in a speech upon the treaty of annexation, which was then pending in the Senate, deliberately and plausibly undertook to convince the Democracy of the free States that the annexation of Texas, so far from being the means of perpetuating slavery, or of strengthening its influence, would, under Providence, be the means of relieving the Northern slave States of that terrible incubus upon their prosperity. I propose to read some extracts from that notable speech, which was delivered on the 4th of June, 1844. Mr. Buchanan said:

"In arriving at the conclusion to support this treaty, I had to encounter but one serious obstacle, and this was the question of slavery. Whilst I ever have maintained, and ever shall maintain, the constitutional rights of the Southern States over their slave property, I yet feel a strong repugnance, by any act of mine, to extend the present limits of the Union over a new slaveholding territory. After mature reflection, however, I overcame these scruples, and now believe the acquisition of Texas will be the means of limiting, not enlarging, the dominion of slavery. There is nothing rash in the counsels of the Almighty. May not, then, the acquisition of Texas be the means of gradually drawing the slaves far to the South, to a climate more congenial to their nature; and may they not finally pass off into Mexico, and there mingle with a race where no prejudice exists against their color? That the acquisition of Texas would, ere long, convert Maryland, Virginia, Kentucky, Missouri, and probably others of the more northern slave States, into free States, I entertain not a doubt. From the very best information, it is no longer profitable to raise wheat, rye, and corn, by slave labor. Where these articles are the only staples of agriculture, in the pointed and expressive language of Mr. Randolph, 'If the slave does not run away from his master, the master must run away from the slave.'"

This was Mr. Buchanan's declaration. Mr. Robert J. Walker, then a Senator from Mississippi, in a public letter, extensively circulated at the North, said:

"The question is asked, Is slavery never to disappear from the Union? This is a startling and momentous question, but the answer is easy, and the proof is clear. *It will certainly disappear, if Texas is reannexed to the Union.*"

Mr. President, it may seem harsh for me to charge that these statements were fraudulently made, with the intent to impose upon and deceive the Northern Democracy. That thousands upon thousands of them, myself among the number, were misled and betrayed, by assurances from such high authority, into the support of the measure for the annexation of Texas, there can be no doubt; and I should like to have some one explain to me how they could have been truthfully and honestly made, when the very treaty for the annexation of Texas, with all the correspondence, was at that time before the Senate, and the occasion of the speech of Mr. Buchanan, from which I have quoted. The negotiation of the treaty was placed solely upon the ground that Great Britain was about to exert her influence to procure the abolition of slavery in Texas. All the schemes of the slave power, in carrying slaves into Texas against the Mexican law and encouraging the revolt against Mexico, were about to be thwarted. Mr. Buchanan and Mr. Walker and the Senate knew very well that it was only because slavery was endangered in Texas, that the treaty was concluded in such hot haste.

I shall take the liberty of reading such extracts from the correspondence as will prove the truth of my assertions.

Mr. Murphy was the chargé from this Government to Texas; and, in a letter addressed to him by Mr. Upshur, Secretary of State, dated Washington, August 8, 1843, he said:

"Sir: A private letter from a citizen of Maryland, then in London, contains the following passage:

"'I learn, from a source entitled to the fullest confidence, that there is now here a Mr. Andrews, deputed by the Abolitionists of Texas to negotiate with the British Government; that he has seen Lord Aberdeen, and submitted his *projet* for the abolition of slavery in Texas; which is, that there shall be organized a company in England, who shall advance a sum sufficient to pay for the slaves now in Texas, and receive in payment Texas lands; that the sum thus advanced shall be paid over as an indemnity for the abolition of slavery; and I am authorized by the Texan minister to say to you, that Lord Aberdeen has agreed that the British Government will guaranty the payment of the interest on this loan, upon condition that the Texan Government will abolish slavery.'

"The writer professes to feel entire confidence in the accuracy of this information. He is a man of great intelligence, and well versed in public affairs. Hence I have every reason to confide in the correctness of his conclusions.

"A movement of this sort cannot be contemplated by us in silence. Such an attempt upon any neighboring country would necessarily be viewed by this Government with very deep concern; but when it is made upon a nation whose territories join the slaveholding States of our Union, it awakens a still more solemn interest. It cannot be permitted to succeed without the most strenuous efforts on our part to arrest a calamity so serious to every part of our country.

"But there is another view of this subject still more important to us, and scarcely less important to Texas herself. The establishment, in the very midst of our slaveholding States, of an independent Government, forbidding the existence of slavery, and by a people born, for the most part, among us, reared up in our habits, and speaking our language, could not fail to produce the most unhappy effects upon both parties. If Texas were in that condition, her territory would afford a ready refuge for the fugitive slaves of Louisiana and Arkansas, and would hold out to them an encouragement to run away, which no municipal regulations of those States could possibly counteract.

In another dispatch, dated January 16, 1844, he says:

"But this is not all. If Texas should refuse to come into our Union, measures will instantly be taken to fill her territory with emigrants from Europe. Extensive arrangements for this are already made, and they will be carried into effect as soon as the decision of Texas shall be known. These emigrants will bring with them European feelings and European opinions. Emigration from the United States will cease; at all events, the people of the Southern States will not run the hazard of subjecting their slave property to the control of a population who are anxious to abolish slavery. Texas will soon cease to be an American State. Her population, her politics, and her manners, will stamp her as European. This fact alone will destroy the sympathy which now exists between that country and this.

"But the first measure of the new emigrants, as soon as they shall have sufficient strength, will be to destroy that great domestic institution upon which so much of the prosperity of our Southern country depends. To this England will stimulate them, and she will also furnish the means of accomplishing it. I have commented upon this topic in the dispatch to Mr. Everett. I will only add, that if Texas should not be attached to the United States, she cannot maintain that institution ten years, and probably not half that time."

The treaty was concluded; and I have but one extract more to read, which is the reason assigned to the Mexican Government, by Mr. Calhoun, who had succeeded as Secretary of State, for the action of this Government. It is dated April 19, 1844:

"In making the fact known to the Mexican Government, the President enjoins it on you to give it, in the first place, the strongest assurance that, in adopting this measure, our Government is actuated by no feelings of disrespect or indifference to the honor or dignity of Mexico, and that it would be a subject of great regret if it should be otherwise regarded by its Government. And, in the next place, that the step was forced on the Government of the United States in self-defence, in consequence of the policy adopted by Great Britain in reference to the abolition of slavery in Texas. It was impossible for the United States to witness with indifference the efforts of Great Britain to abolish slavery there. They could not but see that she had the means in her power, in the actual condition of Texas, to accomplish the objects of her policy, unless prevented by the most efficient measures; and that, if accomplished, it would lead to a state of things dangerous in the extreme to the adjacent States, and the Union itself. Seeing this, this Government has been compelled, by the neccessity of the case, and a regard to its constitutional obligations, to take the step it has, as the only certain and effectual means of preventing it. It has taken it in full view of all possible consequences, but not without a desire and hope that a full and fair disclosure of the causes which induced it to do so would prevent the disturbance of the harmony subsisting between the two countries, which the United States is anxious to preserve."

Mr. President, the war which Mexico had taken the precaution to assure our Government would be the consequence of the annexation, followed immediately; and an appeal was made to the patriotism of the Northern Democracy to stand by the flag of the country. This call was promptly responded to; but the outraged Democracy of the North, now fully conscious of the ulterior designs of the slave power to extend that blighting institution across the continent, to the shores of the Pacific, with almost entire unanimity determined to plant themselves on the platform of Jefferson, and in the first appropriation which was made by the popular branch of the Government, they appended to it the Wilmot proviso; which required that in all the territory to be acquired, as the result of that war, slavery should be forever prohibited, except for the punishment of crime.

Mr. President, of the noble stand taken by the people and the Democracy of the North in that crisis, I desire to make a record. They were true to the instincts of freedom, and they spoke out heartily everywhere in favor of the precepts and the example of Jefferson, and against the spread of human bondage. At that time the Democratic party was in the ascendant in nearly all of the free States, and the very name produced a talismanic effect, because it was believed to be in sympathy with the laboring masses. I begin with the State of Michigan, at that

time one of the strongest and most reliable Democratic States in the Union. In 1847, her Legislature resolved:

"That, in the acquisition of any new territory, whether by purchase, conquest, or otherwise, we deem it the duty of the General Government to extend over the same the ordinance of 1787, with all its rights and privileges, conditions and immunities."

In 1849, the following resolutions, offered by Hon. E. H. Thomson, were adopted:

"*Resolved by the Senate and House of Representatives of the State of Michigan*, That we consider the result of the late war with Mexico, in the acquisition of the Territories of New Mexico and California, as an enduring monument to the honor of our gallant army, regulars and volunteers, officers and soldiers; and that we rejoice in the prospect of extending over that country the beneficent laws and institutions of a free people.

"*Resolved*, That we are in favor of the fundamental principles of the ordinance of 1787; and although we respect the opinions of many eminent statesmen and jurists, that slavery is a mere local institution, which cannot exist without positive laws authorizing its existence, yet we believe that Congress has the power, and that it is their duty, to prohibit, by legislative enactment, the introduction or existence of slavery within any of the Territories of the United States, now or hereafter to be acquired.

"*Resolved*, That our Senators in Congress be instructed, and our Representatives requested, to use all honorable means to accomplish the objects expressed in the foregoing resolution; and that the Governor of this State be requested to forward copies of these resolutions to our Senators and Representatives in Congress."

In the same year, the Democratic State Convention, which nominated a Governor and State officers, passed unanimously the following:

"*Resolved*, That we are opposed to the extension of slavery into the Territories of New Mexico and California, believing them to be now free in virtue of the laws of Mexico, and that its establishment in either of those Territories ought to be prevented."

In the year 1847, the Legislature of New Hampshire, then largely Democratic, resolved:

"That in all territory which shall hereafter be added to, or acquired by, the United States, where slavery does not exist at the time of such addition or acquirement, neither slavery nor involuntary servitude, except for the punishment of crime, whereof the party has been duly convicted, ought ever to exist, but the same should ever remain free; and we are opposed to the extension of slavery over any such territory; and that we also approve the vote of our Senators and Representatives in Congress in favor of the Wilmot proviso."

In 1848, the Legislature of that State, which had an overwhelming Democratic majority, resolved as follows:

"That we are in favor of the passage of a law, by Congress, forever prohibiting slavery in New Mexico and California, and in all other Territories now acquired, or hereafter to be acquired, by the United States, in which slavery does not exist at the time of such acquisition."

And in 1849, the New Hampshire Legislature, still strongly Democratic, unanimously adopted the following resolutions:

"*Resolved by the Senate and House of Representatives, in General Court convened*, That, opposed to every form of oppression, the people of New Hampshire have ever viewed with deep regret the existence of slavery in this Union; that while they have steadfastly supported all sections in their constitutional rights, they have not only lamented its existence as a great social evil, but regarded it as fraught with danger to the peace and welfare of the nation.

"*Resolved*, That while we respect the rights of the slaveholding as well as the free portions of this Union, while we will not willingly consent that wrong be done to any member of the glorious Confederacy to which we belong, we are firmly and unalterably opposed to the extension of slavery over any portion of American soil now free.

"*Resolved*, That, in our opinion, Congress has the constitutional power to abolish the slave trade, and slavery in the District of Columbia; and that our Senators be instructed, and our Representatives be requested, to take all constitutional measures to accomplish these objects."

The Democratic State Committee of New Hampshire, in October, 1847, passed the following resolution:

"*Resolved*, That we declare it our solemn conviction, as the Democratic party have heretofore done, that neither slavery nor involuntary servitude should hereafter exist in any territory which may be acquired by, or annexed to, the United States; and that we approve of the votes of our delegation in Congress in favor of the Wilmot proviso."

In the year 1847, resolutions were passed by the Legislature of Rhode Island

"Against the acquisition of territory, by conquest or otherwise, beyond the present limits of the United States, for the purpose of establishing therein slaveholding States," &c.

By the Legislature of New York:

"That if any territory is hereafter acquired by the United States, or annexed thereto, the act by which such territory is acquired or annexed, whatever such act may be, should contain an unalterable fundamental article or provision, whereby slavery or involuntary servitude, except as a punishment for crime, shall be forever excluded from the territory acquired or annexed."

By the Legislature of New Jersey:

"That the Senators, &c., be requested to use their best efforts to secure, as a fundamental provision to, or proviso in, any act of annexation of any territory hereafter to be acquired by the United States, &c., that slavery or involuntary servitude, except as a punishment for crime, shall be forever excluded from the territory to be annexed."

By the Legislature of Pennsylvania:

"Against any measure whatever, by which territory will accrue to the Union, unless as a part of the fundamental law, upon which any compact or treaty for this purpose is based, slavery or involuntary servitude, except for crime, shall be forever excluded."

By the Legislature of Ohio:

"For the passage of measures in that body, [Congress,] providing for the exclusion of slavery from the Territory of Oregon, and also from any other Territory that now is, or hereafter may be, annexed to the United States."

By the Legislature of Vermont:

"Against the admission into the Federal Union of any new State whose Constitution tolerates slavery."

By the Legislature of Connecticut:

"That if any Territory shall hereafter be acquired by the United States, or annexed thereto, the act by which such Territory is acquired or annexed, whatever such act may be, should contain an unalterable fundamental article or provision whereby slavery or involuntary servitude, except as a punishment for crime, shall be forever excluded from the Territory acquired or annexed."

And in 1850, the following:

"Whereas the people of Connecticut have heretofore, through their Senators and Representatives in General Assembly convened, solemnly and deliberately avowed their purpose to resist, in all constitutional and proper ways, the extension of slavery into the national Territories, and the admission of new slave States into the Federal Union; and also to seek, in a peaceable and constitutional way, the abolishment of the slave trade and of slavery in the District of Columbia; and whereas the important question now before the country touching these matters makes it desirable that these convictions and determinations should be reaffirmed in the most solemn and public manner: Therefore,

"*Resolved*, That Congress has full constitutional power to prohibit slavery in the Territories of the United States by legislative enactment, and that it is the duty of Congress to pass, without unnecessary delay, such strict and positive laws as will effectually shut out slavery from every portion of these Territories."

By the Legislature of Massachusetts, in 1849:

"*Resolved*, That Congress has full power to legislate upon the subject of slavery in the Territories of the Union; that it has freely exercised such power from the adoption of the Constitution to the present time; and that it is its duty to exercise the power for the perpetual exclusion of the institution from those Territories that are free, and for the extinction of the same in Territories where it exists.

"*Resolved*, That, when Congress furnishes governments for the Territories of California and New Mexico, it will be its duty to establish therein the fundamental principle of the ordinance of 1787 upon the subject of slavery, to the end that the institution may be perpetually excluded therefrom, beyond every chance and uncertainty."

At a State Convention of the Democratic party in Massachusetts, composed of more than six hundred members, in 1849, the following resolutions, introduced by Hon. B. F. Hallett, then chairman of the National Democratic Committee, and of the State Democratic Committee, were adopted unanimously, as appears from the Boston *Post*, the organ of the party in New England:

"*Resolved*, That we are opposed to slavery in every form and color, and in favor of freedom and free soil wherever man lives, throughout God's heritage.

"*Resolved*, That, by common law and common sense, as well as by the decision of the Supreme Court of the United States, (in Prigg *vs.* Pennsylvania, 16 Peters,) 'the state of slavery is a mere municipal regulation, founded upon and limited to the verge of the territorial law;' that is, the limits of the State creating it.

"*Resolved, therefore*, That, as slavery does not exist by any municipal law in the new Territories, and Congress has no power to institute it, the local laws of any State authorizing slavery can never be transported there; nor can slavery exist there but by a local law of the Territories, sanctioned by Congress."

This, sir, is pretty good Republican doctrine, coming from high Democratic authority.

In 1848, the Legislature of Ohio resolved:

"That the provisions of the ordinance of Congress of 1787, so far as the same relates to slavery, should be extended to any territory that may be acquired from Mexico by treaty or otherwise."

In 1849, Illinois resolved:

"That our Senators in Congress be instructed, and our Representatives requested, to use all honorable means in their power to procure the enactment of such laws by Congress for the government of the countries and Territories of the United States, acquired by the treaty of peace, friendship, limits, and settlement, with the Republic of Mexico, concluded February 2, A. D. 1848, as shall contain the express declaration 'that there shall be neither slavery nor involuntary servitude in said Territories, otherwise than in the punishment of crimes, whereof the party shall have been duly convicted."

The same year, the following was adopted in Wisconsin:

"That our Senators in Congress be, and they are hereby, instructed, and our Representatives requested, first, to oppose the passage of any act for the government of New Mexico and California, or any other Territory now belonging to the United States, or which may hereafter be acquired, unless it shall contain a provision forever prohibiting the introduction of slavery or involuntary servitude into said Territories, except as a punishment for crimes; second, to oppose the admission of any more slave States into the Federal Union."

In 1850, the following was adopted by the General Assembly of the State of Indiana:

"That our Senators in Congress be instructed, and our Representatives requested, so to cast their votes and extend their influence as to have engrafted upon any law that may be passed for the organization of the Territory recently acquired from Mexico, a provision forever excluding from such territory slavery and involuntary servitude, otherwise than in the punishment of crimes, whereof the party has been duly convicted."

By the Legislature of New York:

"*Resolved*, That the determination indicated by the Governors' messages and resolutions of the Legislatures of various of the slaveholding States, and by the Representatives of such States in Congress, to extend domestic slavery over the territory acquired by the late treaty of peace with the Republic of Mexico, we feel bound to oppose by all constitutional means; and recognising the constitutional power of Congress to prohibit, by positive enactment, the extension of slavery into free territory, our Senators in Congress are hereby instructed and our Representatives reqested to use their best efforts to insert such a positive prohibition into any law they may pass for the government of the Territories in question."

In 1847, Governor Dana, of Maine, a prominent Democrat, in his message to the Legislature, in speaking of the *right* of slaveholders to hold their slaves in the Territories, said:

"On the other hand, the slave States claim that this territory will be acquired, if acquired at all, by the blood and treasure of all the States of the Union, to become the joint property of all; to be held for the benefit of all. And they emphatically ask, 'Is it consistent with justice?' His right to acquire and possess property is one of the inherent rights of man, independent of laws and Constitutions. Not so with the right to his slave; that is an unnatural, an artificial, a statute right; and when he voluntarily passes with a slave to a Territory, where the statute recognising the right does not exist, then at once the right ceases to exist. The slave becomes a free man, with just as much right to claim the master, as the master to claim the slave."

In 1849, the Democratic party in Maine held a State Convention, at which Hon. John Hubbard was nominated for Governor. This Convention was composed of six hundred delegates, at which the following resolution was passed, only one solitary member voting against it:

"*Resolved*, That the institution of human slavery is at variance with the theory of our Government, abhorrent to the common sentiment of mankind, and fraught with danger to all who come within the sphere of its influence; that the Federal Government possesses adequate power to inhibit its existence in the Territories of the Union; that the constitutionality of this power has been settled by judicial construction, by cotemporaneous expositions, and by repeated acts of legislation; and that we enjoin upon our Senators and Representatives in Congress to make every exertion, and employ all their influence, to procure the passage of a law forever excluding slavery from the Territories of California and New Mexico."

And the Legislature, largely Democratic, passed the following:

"*Resolved*, That the sentiment of this State is profound, sincere, and almost universal, that the influence of slavery upon productive energy is like the blight of mildew; that it is a moral and social evil; that it does violence to the rights of man, as a thinking, reasonable, and responsible being. Influenced by such considerations, this State will oppose the introduction of slavery into any territory which may be acquired as an indemnity for claims upon Mexico."

At a State Convention in Pennsylvania, Colonel Samuel Black, of Pittsburgh, offered the following resolution, which was adopted unanimously:

"*Resolved*, That the Democratic party adheres now, as it ever has done, to the Constitution of the country. Its letter and spirit they will neither weaken nor destroy; and they re-declare that slavery is a domestic local institution of the South, subject to State legislation alone, and with which the General Government has nothing to do. Wherever the State law extends its jurisdiction, the local institution can continue to exist. Esteeming it a violation of State rights to carry it beyond State limits, we deny the power of any citizen to extend the area of bondage beyond its present dominion; nor do we consider it a part of the compromises of the Constitution, that slavery should forever travel with the advancing columns of our territorial progress."

This same Colonel Black is now Governor of Nebraska, and recently vetoed a bill, which had been passed by the Legislature, prohibiting slavery in that Territory. The exact *progress* of Democracy in eleven years is here made quite apparent.

The Democratic members of the Legislature of the State of New York, in 1848, in a series of resolutions, included the following:

"*Resolved*, That while the Democracy of New York will faithfully adhere to all the compromises of the Constitution, and maintain all the reserved rights of the States, they declare—since the crisis has arrived when that question must be met—their uncompromising hostility to the extension of slavery in territory now free, which has been or may be hereafter acquired, by any action of the Government of the United States."

Similar resolutions were adopted the same year at Utica, in which Hon. John Van Buren and Hon. JOHN COCHRANE participated.

At a State Convention of the Democratic party of Ohio, in the year 1848, the following resolution was adopted:

"*Resolved*, That the people of Ohio now, as they have always done, looking upon the institution of slavery as an evil, unfavorable to the full development of our institutions; and that, entertaining these sentiments, they will feel it to be their duty to use all the powers consistent with the national compact, to prevent its increase, to mitigate, and finally *eradicate* it."

Want of time, Mr. President, compels me to omit many similar resolutions of State Legislatures and Democratic Conventions; but I wish to call the attention of the Senate and of the country to one more Democratic authority in favor of the prohibition of slavery in the Territories. It is that of the distinguished and lamented Silas Wright. In a letter written by him, dated the 15th of April, 1847, he uses this emphatic language:

"If the question had been propounded to me at any period of my public life, shall the arms of the Union be employed to conquer or the money of the Union be used to purchase territory now constitutionally free, for the purpose of planting slavery upon it? I should have answered, no! And this answer to this question is the Wilmot proviso, as I understand it. I am surprised that any one should suppose me capable of entertaining any other opinion, or giving any other answer as to such a proposition."

Mr. President, the Democratic Representatives from the free States responded with great unanimity to the wishes and instructions of their constituents. Among the distinguished Representatives of the party who voted for the Wilmot proviso in the war appropriation, and in its application to the organization of Oregon Territory, may be mentioned Hon. R. McClelland, Senators Felch and Stuart, of Michigan; Senators Dix and Dickinson, of New York; Allen, of Ohio; Bright, of Indiana; Douglas and Breese, of Illinois; Dodge, of Wisconsin; Brodhead, of Pennsylvania; Atherton and Norris, of New Hampshire; Bradbury and ex-Governor Dunlap, of Maine; Benton, of Missouri; and Houston, of Texas. General Cass expressed his great regret that the hour of adjournment in 1846 arrived before he could record his vote in its favor; and in 1847, he made a speech upon the subject, in which he doubted the expediency of its adoption at that time, and said:

"It would be quite in season to provide for the government of territory not yet acquired from foreign countries after we shall have obtained it."

With the aid of these timid counsels, and the patronage and influence of the Administration, the slave power gained a temporary advantage by the postponement of the measure, and time to concoct new schemes to defeat it. The Presidential election of 1848 was approaching. It is well known that several Northern Democratic politicians were aspirants for the nomination at Baltimore; and among the most prominent were General Cass, of Michigan, and Mr. Buchanan, of Pennsylvania. The plan adopted was to make an onset upon them; to prescribe a new test, as the condition of giving them Southern support, by which their ambitious hopes would all be smothered, unless they changed their opinions. They undertook to debauch our public men, and, with the glittering prize of the Presidency before their eyes, they demanded a surrender of their principles, consent to the expansion of slavery, and submission to the behests of this tyrannical power.

As the State Conventions in Alabama, Virginia, Florida, and Georgia, met to elect delegates to the Baltimore Convention, they passed resolutions, that "under no political necessity whatever" would they give their support to the nominee of the Convention, unless he renounced the heresy that Congress could prohibit the introduction of slavery into the Territories. The State Convention in Georgia met on the 22d of December, and passed the following:

"*Resolved*, That the Democratic party of Georgia will support no man for the office of President or Vice President, who shall not have clearly and unequivocally declared their opposition to the principles of the Wilmot proviso.

"*Resolved*, That it is the constitutional right of every citizen to remove and settle with his *property* into any of the Territories of the United States."

This adroit and well-managed scheme was successful. General Cass could not doubt that "a great change was going on in the public mind," as he admitted there had been in his own; and on the 31st of December, 1847, the Nicholson letter was published in the *Union* newspaper. The Senator from Mississippi says that it was shown about for several days among the Southern members, for their approval. It is also due to truth for me to say that it was read to the Michigan delegation in Congress at that time, and that they unanimously disapproved both of its principles and of the policy of promulgating it. I am sorry to be obliged to add, that their worst fears were realized.

The Nicholson letter denied the power of Congress to prohibit slavery in the Territories, and claimed a right for the people of the Territories to regulate that and all other internal matters. I will not stop to discuss the doctrine, which, although acquiesced in at the time, is now so unsatisfactory to the propagandists of slavery; but I beg leave to quote one single Southern authority against it. It is that of the celebrated John Randolph.

In the year 1803, a petition was presented to Congress, signed by General Harrison, Governor of the Territory of Indiana, which set forth that he had been requested to call a Convention for the purpose of taking the sense of the whole people upon the subject of suspending, for the period of ten years, the operation of the sixth article of the ordinance which prohibited slavery; that such Convention had met and united in the petition, which declared that more than *nine-tenths* of the inhabitants were of opinion that the enforcement of the said article was prejudicial to their interests. This memorial was referred to a committee, a majority of whom were Southern men, and at the head of which was the distinguished Virginian. On the 2d of March, of the same year, Mr. Randolph reported against the prayer of the petition, and, among other things, said:

"The committee deem it highly dangerous and inexpedient to impair a provision wisely calculated to promote the happiness and prosperity of the Northwestern country, and to give strength and security to that extensive frontier. In the salutary operation of this sagacious and benevolent restraint, it is believed that the inhabitants of Indiana will, at no distant day, find ample remuneration for a temporary privation of labor and emigration."

Sir, the great State of Indiana, with her million and a half of people, and with all the privileges and glory of free institutions, is a witness to-day of the truth of the prediction. What is now the State of Michigan was then included in the

Territory of Indiana; and the people of both of those States will ever hold in grateful remembrance the efforts of the noble Southerner, against "squatter sovereignty," to preserve unimpaired the provision which dedicated that Territory to free men and free labor.

It may also be proper to say, that the question of suffrage and eligibility to office in the Territories has uniformly and invariably been determined by Congress, and that General Cass has since voted for Territorial organizations in which those rights were prescribed and defined by Congress. Is slavery of higher moment or more sacred than the right of suffrage and the eligibility to office? If Congress can determine the one, it surely has the power to arrest the desolating march of the other.

The abandonment of the doctrine so dearly cherished by Jefferson, and which had secured freedom in the great States of the Northwest, brought defeat to General Cass and the Democratic party in 1848, but it installed the slave power in complete control. The Northern section had been caught in the web, and they could not relieve themselves from the thraldom. At first they undertook to quiet the conscience of the people, by the assertion that slavery was the creature of local and positive law, and that it could not obtain a foothold in the Territories until it was there lawfully established; and General Cass, in a speech in his own State, said:

"Slavery is the creature of local law, and can claim neither protection, existence, nor recognition, in the Constitution. Slavery does not and cannot exist in Kansas whilst it remains a Territory. The Constitution neither protects nor recognises slavery in the Territories."

Hon. Henry Clay offered the following resolution in the Senate on the 29th January, 1850:

"*Resolved*, That as slavery does not exist by law, and is not introduced into the territory acquired by the United States from the Republic of Mexico, it is inexpedient for Congress to provide by law either for its introduction into, or its exclusion from, any part of the said territory," &c.

In commending this proposition to the Senate, Mr. Clay said:

"This resolution, sir, proposes, in the first instance, a declaration of two truths—one of law, and the other of fact. The truth of law which it declares is, that there does not exist, at this time, slavery in any portion of the territory acquired by the United States from Mexico. When I say, sir, that it is a truth, I speak my own solemn and deliberate conviction."

Hon. Greene C. Bronson, a distinguished lawyer and jurist of New York, in a letter to Hon. JOHN COCHRANE, in 1848, then a distinguished Free-Soiler of New York, said:

"Slavery cannot exist where there is no positive law to uphold it. It is not necessary that it should be forbidden; it is enough that it is not specially authorized. If the owner of slaves removes with, or sends them into, any country, State, or Territory, where slavery does not exist by law, they will from that moment become freemen, and will have as good a right to command the master as he has to command them. State laws have no extra authority; and a law of Virginia which makes a man a slave there, cannot make him a slave in New York, nor beyond the Rocky Mountains."

Hon. Edward Bates, a distinguished lawyer of Missouri, recently declared he did "not believe that the Constitution, by its proper vigor, carries slavery into all the Territories that may be acquired by the United States. He believes that freedom is the rule, and slavery the exception. He does not believe that slavery can exist in any territory acquired by the United States, except by a positive law of Congress."

The Detroit *Free Press*, which is the organ of the Administration, and of the party, in Michigan, said:

"Slavery cannot go to Kansas or Nebraska, for the all-sufficient reason that there is no law there permitting it. It is a perfectly well-established legal proposition, that slavery is the creature of local law, and that it can nowhere exist except by the force of law."

Democratic authority could be multiplied *ad infinitum* to prove the truth of this position, but the above must suffice. This short-lived doctrine has already been displaced; and the accepted theory now is, that slavery exists in the Territories by virtue of the Constitution.

But, Mr. President, the fatal step had been taken in the surrender of a high principle. Henceforward the Northern Democracy were reduced to a state of vassalage. When the fugitive slave law was passed, they avowed their readiness to do the "dirty work" imposed by their Southern masters. If they evinced the slightest disposition to rebel, a threat to dissolve the Union at once reduced them to submission. At last, when their subjection was deemed complete, the abrogation of that sacred and time-honored Missouri compromise was demanded.

If a prophet had appeared to the honorable Senator from Illinois in 1845, when at Springfield, the capital of his adopted State, he uttered the following beautiful apostrophe to the Missouri compromise, he might have said, with Hazael of old: "But what! is thy servant a dog, that he should do this great thing?"

"The Missouri compromise has been in practical operation for about a quarter of a century, and received the sanction and approbation of men of all parties in every section of the Union. It had allayed all sectional jealousies and irritations growing out of the vexed question, and harmonized and tranquillized the whole country. It had an origin akin to the Constitution, conceived in the same spirit of affection, and calculated to remove forever the only danger which seems to threaten to sever the Union. All the evidences of public opinion seemed to indicate that this compromise had been CANONIZED in the hearts of the American people as a SACRED THING, *which no ruthless hand would ever be reckless enough to disturb.*"

In a speech in the United States Senate, delivered in 1845, Mr. Buchanan said:

"The resolutions went to re-establish the Missouri compromise, by fixing a line within which slavery was to be forever confined. That controversy—the Missouri question—had nearly shaken this Union to its centre in an earlier and better period of our history; but this compromise, should it now be re-established, would prevent the recurrence of similar dangers hereafter. Should this question be now left open for one or two years, the country would be involved in one continued struggle. We should witness a feverish excitement in the public mind. Parties would divide on the dangerous and exciting question of abolition, and the irritation would reach such an extreme as to endanger the existence of the Union itself; but close it now, and it would be closed forever. Was it desirable again to have the Missouri question brought home to the people, to goad them to fury? That great question between the two great interests of our country had been well discussed and decided in the Missouri compromise, and from that moment he had sat down his foot on the solid ground then established, and there he would let the question stand forever. Who could complain of the terms of that compromise?"

In a letter of Mr. James Buchanan, dated Washington, August 25, 1847, directed to a Harvest Home of the Democracy of Berks county, Pennsylvania, I find this language:

"After Louisiana was acquired from France, by Mr. Jefferson, and when the State of Missouri, which constituted a part of it, was about to be admitted into the Union, the Missouri question arose, and, in its progress, threatened the dissolution of the Union. This was settled by the men of the last generation, as other important and dangerous questions have been settled, in a spirit of mutual concession. Under the Missouri compromise, slavery was 'forever prohibited' north of 36° 30′; and south of this parallel, the question was left to be decided by the people. Congress, in the admission of Texas, following in the footsteps of their predecessors, adopted the same rule; and, in my opinion, the harmony of the States, and even the security of the Union itself, require that the line of the Missouri compromise should be extended to any new territory which we may acquire from Mexico."

Again, in the same letter, he says:

"Such has been my individual opinion, openly and freely expressed, ever since the commencement of the present unfortunate agitation; and, of all places in the world, I prefer to put them on record before the incorruptible Democracy of old Berks. I therefore beg leave to offer you the following sentiment:

"The Missouri compromise: its adoption, in 1820, saved the Union from threatened convulsion. Its extension, in 1848, to any new territory which we may acquire, will secure the like happy results."

The ostensible reason for the repeal of the Missouri compromise was its alleged unconstitutionality. To this it may be said that, in 1820, it received the sanction of an able Congress, and was approved by Mr. Monroe and all his Cabinet—a majority, as usual, being composed of Southern men; that the provision excluding slavery north of the line of 36° 30′ was re-enacted in the resolutions annexing Texas in 1845, and approved by Mr. Tyler and all his Southern Cabinet; that, upon the bill for the organization of the Territory of Oregon, in 1848, it was proposed as an amendment by the honorable Senator from Illinois, [Mr. DOUGLAS,] and voted for by the following Senators: Messrs. Atchison, Benton, Badger, Bell, Berrien, Borland, Bright, Butler, Calhoun, Davis, Dickinson, Douglas, Downs, Fitzgerald, Foote, Hannegan, Houston, Hunter, Johnson of Maryland, Johnson of Louisiana, Johnson of Georgia, King, Lewis, Mangum, Mason, Metcalf, Pierce, Sebastian, Spruance, Sturgeon, Turney, and Underwood—nearly all Democrats, and Southern men. In the House of Representatives it received eighty-two votes, among which I find the names of Messrs. Bocock, Albert G. Brown, Burt, Clingman, Howell Cobb, Iverson, Andrew Johnson, R. W. Johnson, G. W. Jones, McDowell, McLane, Phelps, Stephens of Georgia, Rhett, Jacob Thompson, and Toombs. It was also voted for in 1850 by most of the distinguished men whose names I have just repeated.

No pretext was urged for the repeal of the Missouri restriction, that it was asked for by the people of the Territory. Every possible demonstration was given, that it was repugnant to the feelings of the people in the free States. In my judgment, it was passed to appease the inexorable demand of the slave interest for dominion. As Ahab coveted Naboth's vineyard, so did the propagandists of slavery cast a longing, wistful look upon the great plains of Kansas.

I will not detain the Senate, Mr. President, with a recital of the atrocious and persistent efforts for years to establish slavery in Kansas, up to that culmination of villainy, the Lecompton Constitution. It is sufficient for me to say, that the unequal struggle of the friends of freedom upon those blood-stained fields was worthy of the best days of the Revolution; and that the Democratic party of the North had become so completely demoralized and debauched, that they neither felt nor dared to express the slightest sympathy for their brethren, who were contending for their rights against the brutal mob of border ruffians, and the power and influence of the Administration. Their distinguished leader and candidate for the Presidency, the honorable Senator from Illinois, [Mr. DOUGLAS,] has avowed, upon the floor of the Senate, that "it was a matter of perfect indifference to him, whether slavery is voted in or out;" and his followers, unmoved by the love of humanity or national glory, are apparently alike indifferent.

Thus, step by step, Mr. President, has the Democratic party of the North ceased to be the party of freedom, and been brought under perfect subjugation to the interests of slavery. If anything were wanting to complete the record of its degradation, and the total abandonment of all its former principles and leaders, it is the voluntary offer, made at Charleston, to submit to and be guided by the political opinions of the Supreme Court, as well to those already promulgated, as to those which they may hereafter declare. For many years the slave power has been adroitly managing to mould and fashion the Supreme Court, so as to bring it into complete subserviency to their interests. There is but one friend of freedom left on the bench—all the other judges are pro-slavery. So constituted, this court has declared that slaves are property under the Constitution, and that they can be lawfully held in any of the Territories. This opinion, in my judgment, is entitled to no more respect than that of the same number of men in this Chamber, or anywhere else; but when we look at the necessary consequence of declaring slaves property under the United States Constitution, and to what must inevitably be the next decision, the right to hold them in the *States*, in defiance of State authority, a voluntary engagement to be bound by such decision is equivalent to a surrender of the whole country to slavery.

The present purposes of the slave power are frankly disclosed in the following article, which appeared in the *Union* newspaper of this city, the organ of the Administration, on the 17th November, 1857:

"The Constitution declares that 'the citizens of each State shall be entitled to all the privileges and immunities of citizens in the several States.' Every citizen of one State coming into another State has, therefore, a right to the protection of his person, and that property which is recognised as such by the Constitution of the United States, any law of a State to the contrary notwithstanding. So far from any State having a right to deprive him of this property, it is its bounden duty to protect him in its possession.

"If these views are correct—and we believe it would be difficult to invalidate them—it follows that all State laws, whether organic or otherwise, which prohibit a citizen of one State from settling in another, and bringing his slave property with him; and most especially declaring it forfeited, are direct violations of the original intention of a Government which, as before stated, is the protection of person and property, and of the Constitution of the United States, which recognises property *in slaves*, and declares that 'the citizens of each State shall be entitled to all the privileges and immunities of citizens in the several States,' among the most essestial of which is the protection of person and property."

Mr. President, the great thought, which overburdened the heart of Jefferson in his latter days, was the usurpations of the Supreme Court. I quote a few of his prophetic warnings, and trust that the people will heed them:

*Extract of a letter to Judge Roane, dated Poplar Forest, September* 6, 1819.

"In denying the right they usurp of exclusively explaining the Constitution, I go further than you do, if I understand rightly your quotation from the Federalist, of an opinion that 'the judiciary is the last resort in relation to the other departments of the Government, but not in relation to the rights of the parties to the compact under which the Judiciary is derived.' If this opinion be sound, then, indeed, is our Constitution a complete *felo de se*. For, intending to establish three departments, co-ordinate and independent, that they might check and balance one another, it has given, according to this opinion, to one of them alone the right to prescribe rules for the government of the others; and to that one, too, which is unelected by and independent of the nation. * * *

"The Constitution, on this hypothesis, is a mere thing of wax in the hands of the Judiciary, which they may twist and shape into any form they please. It should be remembered, as an axiom of eternal truth in politics, that whatever power, in any Government, is independent, is absolute also; in theory only at first, while the spirit of the people is up, but in practice as fast as that relaxes. Independence can be trusted nowhere but with the people in mass. They are inherently independent of all but moral law. My construction of the Constitution is very different from that you quote. It is, that each department is truly independent of the others, and has an equal right to decide for itself what is the meaning of the Constitution in the cases submitted to its action."

*Extract from a letter to Thomas Ritchie, dated Monticello, December* 25, 1820.

"The Judiciary of the United States is the subtle corps of sappers and miners, constantly working under ground to undermine the foundations of our confederated fabric. They are construing our Constitution from a co-ordination of a general and special Government, to a general and supreme one alone. * * * We already see the power, installed for life, responsible to no authority, (for impeachment is not even a scarecrow,) advancing with a noiseless and steady pace to the great object of consolidation. The foundations are already deeply laid, by their decisions, for the annihilation of constitutional State rights, and the removal of every check, every counterpoise, to the engulfing power, of which themselves are to make a sovereign part. * * * That there should be public functionaries independent of the nation, whatever may be their demerit, is a solecism, in a Republic, of the first order of absurdity and inconsistency."

Equally impressive and eloquent was John Randolph, who said:

"But, sir, if you pass the law, the judges are to put their veto upon it by declaring it unconstitutional. Here is a new power, of a dangerous and uncontrollable nature, contended for. The decision of a constitutional question must rest somewhere. Shall it be confided to men immediately responsible to the people, or to those who are irresponsible? for the responsibility by impeachment is little less than a name. From whom is a corrupt decision most to be feared? To me it appears that the power which has the right of passing, without appeal, on the validity of your laws, is your sovereign. * * * But, sir, are we not as deeply interested in the true exposition of the Constitution as the judges can be? With all due deference to their talents, is not Congress as capable of forming a correct opinion as they are? Are not its members acting under a responsibility to public opinion which can and will check their aberrations from duty?"

Nathaniel Macon, of North Carolina, said:

"According to some gentlemen, we were to regard the Judiciary more than the law, and both more than the Constitution. It was a misfortune the judges were not equal in infallibility to the God who made them. The truth was, if the judge was a party man out of power, he would be a party man in. The office would not change human nature."

Now, Mr. President, let me quote from General Jackson, in his veto of the bank bill:

"If the opinion of the Supreme Court covered the whole ground of this act, it ought not to control the co-ordinate authorities of this Government. The Congress, the Executive, and the court, must each for itself be guided by its own opinion of the Constitution. Each public officer, who takes an oath to support the Constitution, swears that he will support it as he understands it, and not as it is understood by others. It is as much the duty of the House of Representatives, of the Senate, and of the President, to decide upon the constitutionality of any bill or resolution which may be presented to them for passage or approval, as it is of the

Supreme judges, when it may be brought before them for judicial decision. *The opinion of the judges has no more authority over Congress than the opinion of Congress over the judges;* and, on that point, the President is independent of both. The authority of the Supreme Court must not, therefore, be permitted to control the Congress or the Executive when acting in their legislative capacities, but to have only such influence as the force of their reasoning may deserve."

General Jackson was aware that he had taken a strong position in that case; and he closes, most solemnly, with an appeal to his Creator. He says:

"I have now done my duty to my country. If sustained by my fellow-citizens, I shall be grateful and happy; if not, I shall find, in the motives which impel me, ample grounds for contentment and peace."

I do not expect to make my case any stronger; but there is an "old public functionary," who now occupies the White House, whose opinions were once entitled to some respect. I wish to contrast them, to show the degeneracy of the times, and especially of the Democratic party.

In a speech in the United States Senate, July 7, 1841, on the bank question, Mr. Buchanan said:

"Now, if it were not unparliamentary language, and if I did not desire to treat all my friends on this (Whig) side of the House with the respect which I feel for them, I would say that the question having been settled so as to bind the consciences of members of Congress when voting on the present bill, is ridiculous and absurd. If all the judges and all the lawyers in Christendom had decided in the affirmative, when the question is brought home to one as a legislator, bound to vote for or against a new charter, upon oath to support the Constitution, I must exercise my own judgment. I would treat with profound respect the arguments and opinions of judges and constitutional lawyers; but if, after all, they fail to convince me that the law was constitutional, I should be guilty of perjury before high Heaven if I voted in its favor.

"But even if the Judiciary had settled the question, I should never hold myself bound by their decision, while acting in a legislative character. Unlike the Senator from Massachusetts, [Mr. Bates,] *I shall never consent to place the liberties of the people in the hands of any judicial tribunal.*"

In the Berks county letter, written in 1847, he said:

"Having urged the adoption of the Missouri compromise, the inference is irresistible that Congress, in my opinion, possesses the power to legislate upon the subject of slavery in the Territories."

In his message to Congress, as President of the United States, he said:

"Slavery existed at that period, (1854,) and still exists, in Kansas, under the Constitution of the United States. This point has at last been firmly decided by the highest tribunal known to our laws. How it could ever have been doubted is a mystery."

And in his letter to Professor Silliman, he reiterated the above, and added:

"Slavery exists in Kansas by virtue of the Constitution of the United States. Kansas is, therefore, as much a slave State as Georgia or South Carolina."

In his last message the President said:

"The right has been established of every citizen to take his property of any kind, *including slaves*, into the common Territories belonging equally to all the States of the Confederacy, and to have it protected there under the Federal Constitution. Neither Congress nor a Territorial Legislature *nor any human power* has any authority to annul or impair this vested right."

Mr. President, I have said enough to prove the *total depravity* of the Democratic party North; the utter abandonment of their principles; their complete and thorough subserviency to Southern dictation. I will not use the harsh language which the Senator from Texas [Mr. WIGFALL] employed the other day, when he said:

"Threaten them, and they will crouch to your feet like so many hounds. Only swear that you are going to dissolve the Union, and the timid creatures will get down on all fours, bite the dust, and kiss the rod raised to chastise them."

But I will say, they have lost the manly, independent spirit, which was the characteristic of the party in the days of General Jackson.

Mr. President, the sentiments of the people of the free States, to whom the acts of their Democratic public servants have been submitted, are well known, and they have been unequivocally expressed. No man has been able to stand up before an enlightened constituency, and justify his betrayal of the interests of free labor. Even the distinguished Senator from Illinois only obtained a majority of his Legislature through an unjust apportionment; the popular majority was against him.

The people of the great Northwestern States, now numbering nearly ten millions of freemen, will ever hold in grateful recollection the memory of those whose statesmanlike and patriotic foresight dedicated the soil upon which they live to free labor; and they are not unmindful of the duty they owe to their posterity. They mean to prove to the world that the same zeal for liberty which inspired their ancestors still animates them. With slavery in the States of this Confederacy, they claim no other right to interfere than to unite with an enlightened Christian world in a public sentiment before which all great wrongs must sooner or later give way. But in the broad Territories of this Union they are determined slavery never shall obtain a foothold. The auction block for fellowmen shall never be established there; the crack of the driver's whip, the clink of the fetter, or the moan of the slave mother at the loss of her offspring, shall never be heard there; but those broad plains, those fertile valleys, and those mountain gorges rich in shining metal, shall be wrought alone by the willing hands of free men. As fast as they are peopled, the school-house and the church will spring up, and civilization and refinement will bring comfort and happiness to the entire population.

Mr. President, a new era is about to dawn upon us; the desperate struggle which has just taken place at Charleston is one of the dying throes of the slave power. The most important functions of this Government—executive, legislative, and judicial—have fallen under its control; and its immense patronage has been arrayed in the unholy work of extending slavery. It must soon surrender the power which it has wielded so despotically over the party in the North and over the whole country. The slave code which these resolutions indicate will never be passed; and the doctrine that slavery exists by virtue of the Constitution of the United States will soon fall into contempt. A party is about to take possession of this Government, with the same name and the same principles of the Republican party of 1800. An enlightened people are thoroughly aroused to the good work; and they will reverse the decisions of your Supreme Court, and the policy which has prevailed under Democratic rule; they will make freedom *national* and slavery *sectional*. Their candidates, LINCOLN and HAMLIN, are thoroughly identified with the interests of the laboring classes, from which they have sprung; and they are thoroughly imbued with the principles and the love of liberty. Around such standard-bearers the hosts of the people will gather, and bear them on to victory. Their inauguration in power will restore the Government to its original design, so beautifully expressed in the preamble to the Constitution, and "form a more perfect Union, establish justice, insure domestic tranquillity, provide for the common defence, and secure the blessings of liberty to ourselves and our posterity."

---

*Published by the Republican Congressional Committee. Price* $1 *per hundred.*

www.ingramcontent.com/pod-product-compliance
Lightning Source LLC
LaVergne TN
LVHW010834120826
845149LV00016B/1373

* 9 7 8 1 4 1 8 1 9 0 2 2 4 *